What

written by Pam Holden

1

Look for pips in this apple.

3

Look for a stone
in this peach.

Look for cheese in this sandwich.

Look for meat
in this pie.

Look for corn
in this husk.

Look for juice in this orange.

Look for nuts
in this shell.

Look for milk in this coconut.